# BASEBALL HALL OF FAMERS

# Ted Williams

### Shaun McCormack

the rosen publishing group's
**rosen central**

Published in 2004 by The Rosen Publishing Group, Inc.
29 East 21st Street, New York, NY 10010

Copyright © 2004 by The Rosen Publishing Group, Inc.

First Edition

**Library of Congress Cataloging-in-Publication Data**

McCormack, Shaun.
Ted Williams / by Shaun McCormack.—1st ed.
    p. cm.—(Baseball Hall of Famers)
Summary: Discusses the life and career of baseball great,
Ted Williams, the Boston Red Sox slugger who has held the
game's highest batting average since 1941.
Includes bibliographical references and index.
ISBN 0-8239-3783-6 (lib. bdg.)
1. Williams, Ted, 1918—Juvenile literature.
2. Baseball players—United States—Biography—Juvenile
literature. [1. Williams, Ted, 1918– 2. Baseball players.]
I. Title. II. Series.
GV865.W5 M33 2003
796.357'092—dc21

                                                      2002012106

*Manufactured in the United States of America*

# Contents

Ted Williams pauses for a moment while taking warm-up swings at Fenway Park, a place he called home for his entire major league career.

# Introduction

It's the last day of the 1941 major league baseball season. Ted Williams, the young Boston Red Sox slugger, is hitting .400. Ted has already clinched the American League batting title. The second place hitter trails him by 50 points.

The Red Sox are getting ready to play a doubleheader. Manager Joe Cronin has given Ted the option to sit out the game to preserve his .400 average.

Ted refuses. He wants to play. He's willing to risk it all in order to raise his average a few more points.

The gamble pays off. Ted goes six for eight in the two games, raising his average to .406. More than sixty baseball seasons have come and gone since 1941, but no one has topped Ted's batting averages.

# Childhood

Theodore Samuel Williams was born on August 30, 1918, in San Diego, California. His mother, May, worked for the Salvation Army. His father, Sam, worked in a photography store. While fighting in the Philippines during the Spanish-American War in 1898, Sam had the honor of riding with former United States president Teddy Roosevelt's cavalry. Ted Williams was named after Teddy Roosevelt, America's twenty-sixth president.

San Diego was a vital location for American naval and marine operations when Ted was growing up. By 1930, military supply depots, hospitals, training stations, and bases had popped up all over the region. Some of Ted's earliest experiences with baseball came from playing pickup games with his friends against navy ballclubs.

San Diego had only about 70,000 residents at the time of Ted Williams's birth. Considered a small town by cosmopolitan East Coasters, San Diego would expand greatly over the next few decades as word spread about its temperate climate.

# Ted's Parents

Most people who have known Ted Williams will describe him as a stubborn, angry man. Later on in life, this earned him the nickname "Terrible Ted." His attitude might have something to do with his childhood.

Ted's mother and father were rarely around when Ted was growing up. His mother worked all day and into the night. His father spent his days and nights working at a photography store on Fifth Avenue in downtown San Diego. Sam Williams rarely got home before nine or ten o'clock in the evening.

May would drag Ted and Danny (Ted's younger brother, born in 1920) with her on her Salvation Army rounds. Her job was to gather donations for San Diego's homeless. People tended to give more if they saw May with her children. Ted did what he could to avoid participating in Salvation Army missions with his mother by playing baseball all day.

May was a popular woman in San Diego. People called her Salvation May, the Sweetheart of San Diego, and the Angel of Tijuana.

May once approached a group of men to ask for a donation for the Salvation Army. None of the men had any money in their pockets. One of them told May that he didn't even have enough money to buy a cup of beer. So May dug into her purse, gave the man 15 cents and said, "Here, let the Army buy you one."

May understood that she could offer a small amount of money to the man in order to

Because San Diego was right across the border from Tijuana, it was easy for citizens to cross over into Mexico and drink during the Prohibition Era. The Salvation Army worked hard to keep late-night revelers and homeless people off the streets.

get a larger donation from him sometime down the road.

Ted grew up reading Salvation Army literature. He internalized the slogans and lived by many of them. Ted loved his mother and respected her work for the Salvation Army. But he was humiliated by it, too. People on the streets in San Diego mocked the Salvation Army uniforms and speeches. Ted was uncomfortable and angry about the looks and slurs directed at his mother and at him.

Ted's sensitivity to the taunts of fans in the baseball stadiums he played in can be traced back to the days when May forced him to walk the streets with her.

Ted wrote in his autobiography, "I was embarrassed that my mother was out in the middle of the street all the time. Until the day she died she did that, and it always embarrassed me and God knows I respected and loved her."

In 1924, the Williams family moved into a six-room apartment on Utah Street. Their new home was very close to the North Park playground in University Heights. Ted spent most of his time in this park playing baseball with his friends. This is where Ted began to develop his baseball skills.

The purchase of the Williams family home seems to have been made possible by a $4,000 loan  to May from a wealthy man named John D. Spreckles, who owned a lot of real estate in San Diego. He let the Williamses live in the house without paying back the

$4,000 loan because of May Williams's charity work for the Salvation Army.

May and Sam kept their distance from each other. Today, the kind of relationship they had would probably end in divorce. But in the 1920s, divorce was considered by most people to be unacceptable. So May and Sam stayed together. As a result, Sam Williams was absent through most of Ted's childhood.

Sam and May's marriage finally fell apart after Ted left home. They split up in 1939 when Sam took a job as an inspector for state prisons.

Ted resented his father. When asked about his middle name—Sam—Ted said it came from his uncle Samuel and not from his own father.

The young Ted Williams was forced to seek fatherly guidance beyond his family. A neighbor named Johnny Lutz, a game warden named Chick Roter, a maintenance worker named Les Cassie, and a high school principal named Floyd Johnson all gave Ted the guidance he might have otherwise gotten from his father.

North Park playground director Rod Luscomb may have been Ted's most important

# The Pacific Coast League

The Pacific Coast League, founded in 1903, sprang from the California State League that dated back to 1886. Temperate West Coast weather made the Pacific Coast League unique. Because it followed a "weather permitting" schedule, some seasons contained as many as two hundred days of play. As a result, there was no way to compare its year-to-year statistics with each other or with leagues that had an established number of games in their season. The league offered exciting, big league baseball to West Coast fans until 1958. But when the Brooklyn Dodgers moved to Los Angeles and the New York Giants took up residence in San Francisco, it was the end for the Pacific Coast League.

male role model. "I tagged after Rod Luscomb almost every day of my life for six or seven years, hanging around like a puppy waiting for him to finish marking the fields or rolling the diamond," Ted is quoted in the book *Ted Williams: A Baseball Life*.

Ted Williams *(back row, second from right)* poses for a picture with his team, the San Diego Padres, in 1937. The Padres belonged to the Pacific Coast League, which was organized in 1903.

Rod Luscomb was a great friend for a young ballplayer. Luscomb took care of the North Park baseball field and helped out Ted when the older kids tried kicking him and his friends off the field.

## Growing Up in San Diego

San Diego might have one of the most comfortable climates in the United States. A San Diego Chamber of Commerce flyer from the early 1920s said the city was "a place where you may be out-of-doors every day and at every hour of the day during the entire year."

So Ted spent his days outside learning how to hit a ball. Ted and his friends played ball before Little League became popular. They played baseball spin-off games, too, like "over-the-line" and "hit-the-bat." They made their own rules and focused on hitting. They hardly ever ran the bases. The games Ted and his friends played were meant to give everyone as many chances to hit as possible.

For Ted, base running was always the hardest part of the game. He had a recurring dream that he had to crawl to home plate on his hands and knees after rounding third base. And while most kids his age worshiped the walloping home runs hit by Babe Ruth for the New York Yankees, Ted's hero was the fast-running Pepper Martin of the St. Louis Cardinals.

San Diego didn't have a professional base-ball team early in the 1930s. So Ted focused his attention on lefty-hitter Bill Terry of the New York Giants. His dream as a kid was to get a hit off of Wilbur Wiley, a neighborhood boy who got the best of Ted until Ted turned fourteen.

In January 1934, Ted went to watch San Diego's Hoover High School varsity baseball team. Coach Wos Caldwell was beginning his spring baseball tryouts. Ted got a chance to see how good the older kids were. The following year, he'd have to compete against them for a starting spot on the Hoover High baseball team.

Ted was only fifteen years old, but he thought he was just as good as the older kids. When he talked Caldwell into letting him take a few swings with the big kids, Ted hit two mammoth shots. One flew past a small park on the high school field where kids ate lunch. Another one smashed into the wall of a building more than 300 feet away. Ted was crushing balls that could clear the fences of major league baseball stadiums before he started high school!

Ted made the varsity team at Hoover High the following year. As a freshman, he played in the outfield and pitched. He hit over .300 in his sophomore year, getting about three hits for every

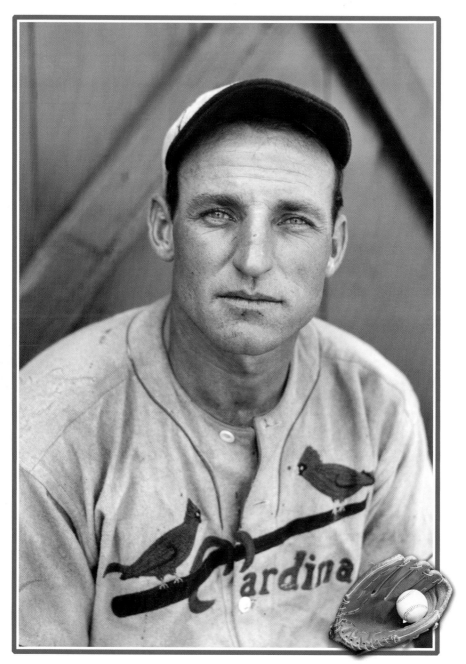

John "Pepper" Martin was a third baseman known for his speed and fiery competitiveness. Although he wasn't a great hitter, or even a very good fielder, his unflagging determination made him Williams's favorite ballplayer.

ten times he came to the plate. Baseball batting averages are calculated by dividing the number of hits by the number of chances at the plate.

Ted crushed the ball repeatedly during his junior year, finishing up with a whopping .538 batting average. He cooled down a bit in his senior year, but he still managed to hit .403.

High school ball was only a small piece of Ted's baseball life. He also played American Legion baseball and pickup games with one of San Diego's military teams. He even played semiprofessional baseball for a team sponsored by a San Diego bakery.

Ted had the chance to earn five dollars a game by playing for the Texas House Liquor team, but May would not let him. May's job was to clear drunks from the streets of San Diego. If Ted played for a baseball team sponsored by a liquor distributor, it would contradict her efforts for the Salvation Army.

During his junior year at Hoover High, Ted started to make a name for himself in baseball. He struck out twenty-three batters while pitching, and he hit a long home run in a game against a high school team from Santa Monica, California. Striking out twenty-three batters in a game is an incredible accomplishment. With nine innings in a game and three outs for each team in an inning, there are twenty-seven outs for each team in a baseball game. This means there were only four times in the entire game when a Santa Monica hitter was able to put the ball in play.

Herb Bennyhoven of the St. Louis Cardinals invited Ted to a tryout camp soon after this game. Ted agreed to the tryout even though he had a sore foot. Uncomfortable at the plate, he didn't impress anyone at the tryout.

Detroit Tigers talent scout Marty Krug had his doubts about the young Ted Williams. Ted stood six feet, three inches tall and weighed just 150 pounds when he was in high school. Major league baseball teams tend to look for bulkier, stronger players. Krug told Ted's mother, "If you let this boy play baseball now, it will kill him."

Krug was wrong.

Ted played American Legion ball throughout his senior year of high school. Scouts from the New York Yankees, St. Louis Cardinals, and his hometown's new team, the San Diego Padres, were following his progress.

Ted was one among a group of prospects who were allowed to practice with the San Diego Padres in the summer of 1936. That summer, Bill Lane brought the Padres to San Diego as part of the Pacific Coast League. The Padres played an exhibition game against the Navy All-Stars on June 23, 1936, and jumped out to a 12–0 lead. Because of this large lead, manager Frank Shellenback put some of his prospects into the game. Most of them were sixteen, seventeen, and eighteen years old. Ted was sent out to play left field. Giving up ten runs, Ted and the other kids almost lost the game for the Padres. But Ted lined a base hit during his only time at the plate.

The Padres' second baseman, Bobby Doerr, remembers the excitement surrounding Ted in San Diego. Padres players had read

Ted Williams slides into home plate during a home game against the Cleveland
Indians in 1946.

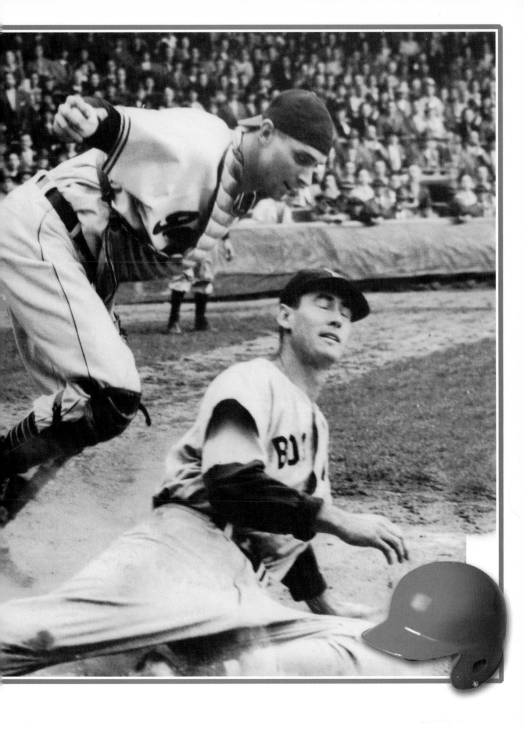

Williams takes his first turn in the batting cage at the beginning of the Red Sox's 1957 spring training in Sarasota, Florida. During the 1956 season, Williams had batted .345.

about him in the San Diego newspapers. They knew how dominating he was on the pitcher's mound and in the batter's box for Hoover High and for his American Legion team.

Doerr said in the book *Ted Williams: A Baseball Life* that he remembered how Ted and other high school kids were working out with the Padres one day at their Lane Field training facility. The high school kids were fielding grounders and shagging fly balls with the Padres. None of the veterans wanted to share the batting cages with the kids. Doerr said one of his teammates looked over at Ted. Then he looked to his teammates and said, "Let the kid hit." Ted was given the chance to show the veterans what he could do. This time, he was comfortable at the plate and crushed several balls over the fence.

Three days later, the Padres signed Ted to a minor league contract.

# 2 The Minor Leagues

The San Diego Padres signed Ted to his first professional baseball contract on June 26, 1936. May and Sam Williams had to sign a parental consent form because their son was only seventeen years old and still a minor. Ted was signed to play for the Padres in the Pacific Coast League for $150 a month. The Padres promised not to trade or sell Ted's contract to any other team until the end of the 1937 season. The Padres were forced into this agreement by May Williams. She did not want her son sent off to a different ballclub in a different city at such a young age.

On June 27, the *San Diego Union* newspaper published details of Ted's contract. In the article, the newspaper reported that Ted was "a diamond," a rare commodity at Herbert Hoover High School. They reported that Ted was one of "the best natural prospects developed in this area in some time."

The Padres' first year in San Diego was 1936. They were wallowing in sixth place with a 37 to 42 record when Ted signed. Ted got his first professional at bat the next day. But he was punched out on a called third strike thrown by Henry "Cotton" Pippen of Sacramento. Ted didn't get much playing time the next few days.

He threw for batting practice during pregame warm-ups. Coach Frank Shellenback's roster was stacked with outfielders. He wanted to see if Ted could pitch. *San Diego Union* sportswriters had always said Ted was much better at the plate than on the pitcher's mound. This held true into Ted's professional career.

Shellenback gave Ted a chance at the plate on July 3, when the Padres were down by ten runs in a game against the Los Angeles Angels. Ted came into the game as a pinch hitter against Los Angeles pitcher Glen Babler and got

With his uniform hanging off his narrow shoulders, Williams's thin frame gave no hint of the sheer power he brought to the plate.

his first hit as a professional. He stayed in the game and lined another single off of Los Angeles relief pitcher Joe Berry.

But Shellenback made the mistake of putting in Ted as a pitcher. He gave up two home runs. One of them was smashed high and deep into the sky and finally fell into a tree 450 feet away! Shellenback had seen enough from Ted as a pitcher, but he was gaining confidence in the kid's ability to hit.

Ted got his first start with the Padres on July 4, 1936, going one for four. It was a double, Ted's first extra base hit. He started in both games of a doubleheader on July 5, but he couldn't get a hit. Shellenback benched Ted again and started looking around for a veteran to fill his spot.

In *My Turn at Bat*, Ted wrote "[Shellenback was] a wonderful, wonderful man, a man I respected as much as any I've known in baseball, but I don't mean to say he was all out for young ballplayers."

Padres owner Bill Lane had special plans for Ted. He wanted to groom the young prospect into a mature ballplayer. He wanted to keep him healthy. Lane hoped to nurture Ted. Teams often sacrifice the future potential of players for the present by forcing them into starting positions before they are ready. The pressure to perform at a professional level over-whelms them. They lose their confidence and turn out to be average ballplayers.

Baseball coaches have learned that the best way to groom a young prospect is to introduce him slowly to the game. If a ballplayer is overcome by pressure, he will usually crumble beneath it. By easing the burden on a youngster, a coach gives the player the chance to learn at his own pace. The less pressure a player feels, the more comfortable he will be. This was Lane's plan for Ted.

It fit well with Shellenback's tactics, too. Shellenback liked to fill his roster with veterans because they were older, more experienced play-ers. He had little patience for rookies and the mistakes they were bound to make. Although younger players usually have more raw talent and can be faster and more enthusiastic, Shellenback had more confidence in experienced veterans than talented rookies.

This led the Padres to sign veteran right-fielder Ivey "Chick" Shiver on July 7. Shiver took over in right field. Left out of the starting lineup, Ted spent most of his time watching the game from the dugout.

Ted stayed on the bench for a month. He got another shot on August 9 when outfielder Sid Durst was injured. Shellenback put Ted into the lineup that day for a doubleheader against the Portland Beavers. Ted played to his potential, lining three hits and driving in two runs, as the Padres won both games. After the two victories, the Padres were just three games out of first place.

*San Diego Union* sportswriter Monroe McConnell had followed Ted's exploits with Hoover High and American Legion ball. He wrote: "Young Ted Williams, Padre recruit who got his chance in the outfield when Sid Durst was out of the lineup temporarily because of a pulled muscle, delivered like a veteran and Padre fans probably will see more of him."

Like Williams, Edward Collins was a great hitter. His style of "choking up" on the bat was adopted by Williams early in his career.

Boston Red Sox talent scout Eddie Collins had been in the stands during the doubleheader. Collins, who had played second base in the professional leagues, was impressed by Ted's ability. He asked Padres owner Bill Lane about Ted. Lane told Collins that he couldn't negotiate Ted's contract until the end of the 1937 season because of the promise he had made to May Williams. Collins convinced Lane to give the Red Sox first choice on Ted's contract when the time came.

A few days later, Ted went zero for seven in a doubleheader and sat on the bench for the rest of August. The Padres were closing in on first-place Portland when right fielder Ivey Shiver broke the news to Coach Shellenback that he was leaving the Padres to coach a football team in Georgia. Shellenback gave Ted the start in left field against a local semipro team on September 1. Going two for three, with a double, a triple, and two RBIs, Ted's performance earned him a fresh start in the lineup.

As a result, Ted got his first taste of a pennant race. He lined a single, crushed a double, and made a jumping catch over the left field fence to steal a home run on September 6 during a game against the Sacramento Solons.

The Padres moved up in the standings during the last week of the 1936 season. They finished one and a half games behind Portland but still made the playoffs. The Padres lost the first game of their playoff series 6–3 to the Oakland Oaks on September 15, but Ted hit his first home run as a professional. The Padres lost the series, four games to one.

Ted finished his first pro season with a .271 batting average. He had lined 8 doubles, 2 triples, and 1 home run in 107 chances at the plate.

# 1937

In 1937, Ted showed up at camp ready to play. He reported to the training facility early so he could work on his fielding with Sid Durst. Ted was bent on becoming an everyday player for the Padres. Wanting the same thing for Williams, team owner Bill Lane gave Durst the responsibility of preparing the rookie for the starting lineup. Durst focused on Ted's fielding. He knew Ted needed very little coaching with his hitting. The Padres didn't want to tamper with Ted's sweet swing.

Ted worked hard at camp, but he still started the season on the bench. On April 11, Ted hit his first home run of the season. On April 27, he hit another homer. Benched again after that, Ted didn't get a consistent spot in the starting lineup until June 22 when he knocked in the winning run against

Portland with a 400-foot inside-the-park homer at Lane Field.

Ted crushed four home runs in the following week. The Padres took over first place in the Pacific Coast League.

By August, Ted was hitting balls over the fence with ease. Coach Shellenback benched Ted on August 20 but used him as a pinch hitter late in the game. Ted hit a home run in the eleventh inning for a win. And he knocked in the winning run in an August 31 game with an eighth-inning homer. He hit two more home runs the next day, too.

The Padres struggled down the stretch but finished with a good record, making the Pacific Coast League playoffs for the second consecutive year. Ted and slugger Tommy Thompson led the Padres through the playoffs. They won eight games in a row and captured the Pacific Coast League championship. It was a great time for Ted, who finished his first full professional season with a .291 batting average. After starting the season on the bench, he had blasted in 23 home runs.

# Breaking Balls

Experienced pitchers judge young hitters by their ability to hit breaking balls, pitches that descend during their travel from the pitcher's hand to home plate. Sliders and curveballs are the most common kinds of breaking balls. High school and semipro pitchers are rarely able to throw breaking balls for strikes. It takes experience and practice for a pitcher to develop the skill.

In high school and semipro ball, hitters hardly ever see good breaking balls. As a result, veteran pro pitchers usually throw rookies nothing but breaking balls because rookies too often swing at them and miss.

But Ted was eating Pacific Coast League fastballs for breakfast. When he started crushing balls over the fence, pitchers started to throw him nothing but breaking balls. Veteran pitchers in the league were talking about the kid. Ted took breaking balls in stride. He was able to lay off them if they fell out of the strike zone. He was able to crush the ones in the strike zone. It seemed he was ready for the major leagues.

Padres owner Bill Lane had kept his promise to May Williams. But once the 1937 season was over, the Padres looked to sell Ted's contract and make some money. Lane kept his word to the Red Sox as well. Lane contacted Red Sox scout Eddie Collins when minor league owners held their 1937 winter meeting. Lane told Collins that he had the first shot at bidding on Ted's contract. The Red Sox were one of five teams interested in signing Ted. The Boston Braves, New York Giants, Detroit Tigers, and Brooklyn Dodgers were interested, too.

The Giants were ready to make a deal with Lane's Padres. But Collins pushed and prodded Red Sox owner Tom Yawkey to buy Ted's contract, and the Red Sox signed Ted for $7,500 over two years.

This doesn't sound like a lot of money today, but it was a pretty good wage for an eighteen-year-old during the Great Depression of the 1930s. At the same time, a future super-star pitcher named Stan Musial was earning

Williams signs his contract with Edward Collins in 1947. Although Collins told reporters, "I've just signed the best ball player in the world—barring none," the Boston press criticized Williams for his constant salary negotiations.

$65 dollars a month in the minor leagues. That is only $780 a year. Ted would earn $3,000 in his first year and $4,500 in his second year.

Compared to most people in that time, Ted was rich.

# The Boston Red Sox

**E**very ballplayer has it tough when he first joins the major leagues. He has to endure heckling from fans and from teammates. He has to deal with his own inexperience. He has to cope with the intimidation of big cities. A rookie who makes it to the majors usually starts off playing against the heroes he had worshiped as a kid. Added together, being a rookie can be pretty unnerving.

This was what Ted faced when he showed up for spring training with the Red Sox in 1938. He was full of doubt. Red Sox fans were full of doubt. His own teammates and coaches were doubtful, too. They knew Ted had a sweet swing, but they didn't know if he was ready to compete in the American League.

Boston, Massachusetts, is located in New England, in the northeast corner of the United States. Ted was from southern California. New Englanders referred to San Diego as Cow Country. They made up nicknames for Ted. Meathead and California were the ones that stuck. Sportswriters for the *Boston Globe* newspaper said Ted's muscles looked like eggs rolled in a handkerchief. They called him California Cracker and San Diego Saparoo. (Saparoo is slang for a gullible fool.)

If the mental abuse wasn't enough, Ted had to deal with the reality that he was not yet physically capable of competing at the major league level. He went zero for four in his first appearance against a major league pitcher.

The next day, the *Boston Globe* printed that Ted "Babyface" Williams was overmatched. "The cocky West Coast youngster is lacking in experience and was easily fooled by [Ira] Hutchinson, who fanned him," the paper reported.

Ted was farmed out to the Minneapolis Millers, one of the Red Sox's minor league clubs. He wasn't surprised. Ted knew he

Rogers Hornsby believed in Williams's talent long before anyone would think of nicknaming Ted "the Splendid Splinter."

needed more time to work on his game. He was just as good as anyone when it came to swinging the bat, but he wasn't ready to hit off of major league pitchers. Ted accepted this and went to Minneapolis with a good attitude.

Ted befriended baseball great Rogers Hornsby during his time with the Millers. Hornsby wanted Ted to think about baseball—the whole game of baseball—not just hitting.

The *Minneapolis Star* newspaper bashed Ted after a spring training game in 1938. He made some rookie mistakes that lost an exhibition game for the Millers. Ted had grounded a pitch and stayed in the batter's box because he assumed the ball would roll foul. But the ball stayed fair and he was thrown out at first. If he had run the ball out, he might have been safe at first base with an infield single. The newspaper called him the "goat of the game" and said he made a "bonehead" play by not running out a ground ball.

Regardless of his rookie mistakes, Ted was penciled into the cleanup spot of the Millers' lineup. Batting cleanup meant Ted would hit fourth. It's called cleanup because the hitter is expected to clean up the bases. He's supposed to knock the runners in. Cleanup hitters usually get a lot of chances to hit with men on base. If they're good, they earn a lot of RBIs.

Millers manager Donie Bush was excited by the idea that Ted would bat fourth. The distance down the line was 280 feet in right field at the Millers' Nicollet Park. This is an incredibly short distance, even for a minor league ballpark. With Ted batting lefty, Bush had dreams of the rookie crushing balls over the fence.

But Ted didn't look good at first, starting the season zero for twelve. He walked five times and lined a single in the season's third game. On April 20, Ted went two for five. Newspapers reported that the Millers were looking for a lefty slugger to beef up their weak lineup.

On April 21, Ted showed his teammates more of his skills when he launched two home runs. One of Ted's home runs traveled 450 feet before it hit the ground, rolled, and came to a stop 512 feet away from home plate. Ted's mighty swings were the only runs the Millers scored that day. They lost the game 6 to 2.

A few games later, Ted hit another 450-foot shot.

Once he started playing well, the fans and the sportswriters started to like him. No one (besides manager Donie Bush) called him Meathead anymore. They were calling him The Kid.

Ted put on a home run show over the next few games. He blasted one high and deep down the right field line at Nicollet Park. The distance to the fence down the right field line was only 280 feet at Nicollet, but the ball landed at least 100 feet past the fence. On May 1, Ted hit two more long balls. The first one traveled about 400 feet. The next one sailed over the fence and landed on the far side of Nicollet Avenue.

People were beginning to compare Ted's home run pace to John Hauser's 1933 season with the Millers. Hauser hit 69 home runs that year. Sportswriters were beginning to wonder if Ted could hit that many.

By May 30, Ted had already hit 12 home runs.

The only thing that dulled Ted's rising star was his inexperience in the outfield. He crushed two more home runs in a game against the Toledo Mudhens but misjudged and dropped a fly ball in the same game. Ted could look awkward and uncomfortable in the outfield.

Millers manager Donie Bush defended Ted's fielding problems, saying it was rare for Ted to make a mistake in the outfield. Ted usually threw to the correct base. He was good at charging ground balls, and he fielded them cleanly. He rarely misjudged fly balls, Bush said.

Although he could not be called a great fielder, Ted Williams was a hard worker.
Here he leaps for a drive hit over his head in Boston.

Ted's manager said sportswriters exploited Ted's miscues in the field. According to Bush, Ted made very few mistakes in right field. He said the writers made it seem like Ted was a weak right fielder when he was just as good as anyone else.

But Bush didn't defend Ted all the time. He said Ted had a short attention span. He mentioned a game when the opponent had the bases loaded and the batter at the plate had a full count. Bush looked into the outfield. He saw Ted with his back to the field, waving at a kid sitting atop a building beyond the fence. There were also times when Bush would look outfield and see Ted practicing his swing. He'd scream at Ted, "Pay attention to the game, ya' meathead!"

By the middle of June, Ted was hitting almost .350 with 20 home runs. Red Sox owner Tom Yawkey was convinced that he'd made a good decision when he signed Ted. He wasn't impressed with the home runs Ted hit at Nicollet Park because it was only 280 feet down the right field line. It was at least 300 feet down the line in most major league parks and Ted was hitting the long ball in every park he played. He wasn't hitting cheap shots, either. He was crushing the ball high into the sky to launch it 450 feet from home plate.

By June 18, Ted was sporting a twenty-one-game hitting streak. Irvin Rudick of the *Minneapolis Star* wrote this about the slugger:

> From the throats of a thousand youngsters, members of the "Knothole Gang," came the chorus: "We want a home run! We want a home run!"
>
> They were calling to Ted Williams, the four-base specialist, and who is Ted to deny these lads their desires?
>
> Williams strode to the plate swinging three bats as though they were hardly more than a bandleader's wand. He chose one to his liking, and hardly had the bat contacted the sphere than these same youngsters, seated in a special section of the left-field stands, rose as one and cheered

Tigers catcher Frank House watches another Williams hit clear the infield. During this 1954 doubleheader against Detroit, Ted got eight hits in nine times at bat, including two home runs and seven RBIs.

Williams all the way around the bases as he smote a mighty home run to send three runs home and give the Millers a 5–3 victory over Toledo at Nicollet Park Saturday afternoon.

It was no ordinary homer that Williams propelled over the right-center wall. The Kid doesn't do things that way. He lashed the pellet to the left of the major league score board and on across Nicollet Avenue, the Ruthian swat traveling fully 440' in the air.

During that 1938 season, Ted continued to wow fans and writers with mammoth shots. The Millers stayed within striking distance of the first-place St. Paul ballclub through the summer. By the end of August, Ted was leading the league with a .360 average, 41 homeruns, and 130 RBIs.

The Millers had a chance to take over first place in early September. They were three games in back of first-place St. Paul. But when they began a four-game series with their rival, the Millers fell apart. They lost three of the four games and finished the season on a sour note.

Ted was in position to break one of the games open. The bases were loaded and he had three balls and one strike. Being ahead in the count is the best thing a hitter can do for himself because he forces the pitcher to come in with a strike. This is especially true when there are men on base. If the pitcher had thrown a ball out of the strike zone, Ted could have watched it go by. He would have earned a walk and forced in a run.

When a hitter is behind in the count, he is at the mercy of the pitcher. He is forced to protect the plate. He has to swing at anything close, or else he runs the risk of being called out on strikes.

When pitcher Lloyd Brown came in with the 3–1 pitch, Ted could have lined the ball into the gap between right field and center field for a double. Instead, his swing was weak and he popped the ball up for an out.

Angry at himself, Ted went into the dugout and punched a glass watercooler.

Mindful of staying off the disabled list, Williams soaks an elbow that was hit by a pitch during a 1946 exhibition game.

Smashing it into hundreds of pieces, he also injured his hand.

The Millers' standings fell over the rest of the season, but Ted had given the fans something to cheer about. He won the Triple Crown Award that year. The Triple Crown Award is given to a player who leads the league in the three most important statistics: batting average, home runs, and runs batted in.

Red Sox management worried. Ted was still rough around the edges and his temper could be a problem. But they were ready to give him a shot in the major leagues.

The Sox released starting outfielder Ben Chapman in the fall of 1938. Chapman had been a good hitter, batting .340 that year and leading the league in stolen bases. Chapman's attitude was his main problem. He argued with Red Sox manager Joe Cronin and owner Tom Yawkey, so they let him go. His departure made room for Ted.

In 1939, Ted was going to be a starting outfielder for the Boston Red Sox.

# Establishing a Reputation in the Major Leagues

**F**ew people doubted Ted's ability to become part of the Red Sox's starting lineup when he went back to Sarasota for spring training camp in 1939. The departure of Ben Chapman left a hole in right field.

It was a very hopeful time for Ted, but a dangerous era for the United States. Military aggression was brewing in Europe. German leader Adolf Hitler's menacing troops were marching through Europe, striking fear into the heart of every Jewish person living within Hitler's reach. It is one of the darkest chapters in world history. While marching through Europe, Hitler's troops built concentration camps where they enslaved, tortured, and murdered Jews. The German army practiced the horrible act of

German chancellor Adolf Hitler holding court with his top Nazi officers. Ted Williams would be drafted to fight against Hitler's forces late in World War II.

genocide against Europe's Jewish population. Genocide is the systematic, premeditated extermination of an entire racial, political, national, ethnic, or religious group.

America was still trying to determine its position toward the European conflict. Millions of Americans were searching for reasons why the country should avoid the fighting. President Franklin Delano Roosevelt had refused to enter the conflict until the infamous Japanese sneak attack on the Pearl Harbor, Hawaii, military base in 1941.

Political and military issues were in the back of Ted's mind when he arrived at training camp in 1939. He was aware of the European conflict. He would later be drafted into the U.S. armed forces and fight in the war.

But for now, he had a job to do. His job was to break into the major leagues.

## Ted and the Press

It is impossible to talk about Ted Williams's career without mentioning the terrible relationship he had with Boston's sportswriters. *Boston Globe* sportswriters had a lot of fun with Ted that spring, mocking him every chance they got. In fact, they never gave up provoking and abusing the hot-tempered slugger throughout his entire career.

In the spring of 1939, Ted was only twenty-one years old and low on self-confidence. He was fidgety and graceless when dealing with the press. Unable to predict how reporters would

A circle of reporters surrounded Williams after a game in 1952. Even though he was Boston's best player for the entirety of his major league career, the city's sports reporters never took a liking to him.

react, he rarely thought about his responses before he spit them out.

Ted's youth and inexperience gave sports-writers the upper hand. It was easy to lure him into making bold or foolish statements. They set him up with questions designed to intimidate him. They provoked him with insults. Ted's hot temper and sharp tongue gave the *Globe* hundreds of eye-popping, controversial stories over the years.

*Globe* reporter Harold Kaese knew that his colleagues planned to draw Ted out and exploit his anger that spring. Kaese tried to warn Ted, telling him that his dealings with the press would define his public image in Boston. Instead of accepting the information for what it was worth, Ted took it as a threat. Ted never got along with Kaese. They had a bitter relationship throughout Ted's career.

## A Tough Spring

The press wasn't Ted's only problem that spring. His parents' marriage had fallen apart. He was happy to leave home, though it was the last time he would spend in the apartment on Utah Street.

Ted was tremendously eager to play baseball in the spring of '39, but a lingering upper respiratory infection kept him down. He was two days late to camp because he had stopped to check into a hospital during the drive in his new car from San Diego to Florida.

The Red Sox had high hopes of battling the New York Yankees for the American League's Eastern Division pennant that season. Unless they were plagued by injuries or disappointing performances from their stars, it looked like the Red Sox would field a strong team.

Sox manager Joe Cronin was counting down the days to a spring exhibition series against the Cincinnati Reds. The Reds had been a powerful team in 1938 and were expected to be one of the National League's best teams in 1939. Cronin thought that the exhibition series his team played with the Reds would show how good the Sox really were.

In the first game of the series with the Reds, Ted hit a 450-foot home run. During the second game, the score shot through the roof. The Sox and Reds were playing in Florence, South Carolina, where tropical storm–force winds were carrying almost every pop-up and fly ball over the fence. The umpires finally called the game off after each team scored 18 runs. Both teams had run out of baseballs!

Ted wasn't able to play in that game. His upper respiratory infection had gotten much worse. Cronin took Williams out of the lineup so he'd be ready for opening day in Boston.

## Ted's First Major League Game

The Sox were scheduled to open the season on April 19 at Yankee Stadium in New York City, but the game was postponed by rain. When the teams laced up their cleats to play the following day, ten future Hall of Famers took the field. In addition to Ted, there were Lou Gehrig, Bill Dickey, Joe Gordon, Red Ruffing, Joe DiMaggio, Lefty Grove, Jimmie Foxx, Bobby Doerr, and the Sox's player-manager, Joe Cronin.

For his first major league game, Ted batted sixth in the Sox lineup. Red Ruffing was

Joe DiMaggio, Mickey Mantle, and Ted Williams stand with their bats on their shoulders in 1956. All of them would eventually be inducted into the Hall of Fame. Still a rookie at the time, Mantle would go on to take over DiMaggio's position in center field.

on the mound for the Yankees. Ted's first major league at bat came in the second inning. Ruffing struck him out. Ted got his second at bat in the fourth inning. This time Ted zoned in on Ruffing's fastball and smashed it deep to right center. The ball bounced off the wall in right-center field at Yankee Stadium, and Ted cruised into second base with a double. It was his first major league hit—something a professional ballplayer always remembers.

With only his trainers as an audience, Williams digs in for another batting practice before a home game at Fenway.

The Sox lost the game 2–0, but Ted had crushed a ball off of one of the league's best pitchers in the legendary Yankee Stadium.

In the field, Ted caught a line drive hit by the legendary Yankee first baseman Lou Gehrig, a future Hall of Famer. It was the first and only game that Ted and Gehrig played against each other. Gehrig, who at one time had played 2,130 consecutive games at first base, played his last major league game on May 2, 1939.

## Getting Comfortable in the Major Leagues

In the Sox's next series at Briggs Stadium in Detroit, Ted did something no slugger had ever done. He blasted a ball completely out of the stadium. He didn't just knock it over the fence, he launched it completely over the third seating deck. The ball flew over the stadium roof, crashing down into a garage door across the street from the ballpark.

The mammoth shot came when Ted was ahead in the count three balls and no strikes.

He knew pitcher Bob Harris would have to come in with a strike. A manager will usually tell a hitter to hold his bat back when a 3–0 pitch is on the way. Most coaches and managers think that when a pitcher falls that far behind in the count, the pitcher has lost the ability to throw his pitches in the strike zone. They don't want their hitters swinging at bad pitches and hitting weak fly balls or grounders when they can take a pitch and earn a base on balls.

Lucky for Ted, Cronin had faith in him. Cronin thought Ted was a disciplined hitter. Ted was usually good at laying off of bad pitches, so Cronin thought Ted would swing only if the pitch was perfect to hit.

Ted was expecting Harris to throw a steamer right down the middle of the plate. And that's exactly what he did. To this day, when people talk about the most legendary home runs ever hit, they talk about the one Ted hit in his first year with the Boston Red Sox.

Ted struggled somewhat after his hot start, but he ended up having a great rookie season. Ted tallied 185 hits. He batted .327 with 31 home runs and 145 RBIs. He drew 107 walks, which is great for a rookie.

But the most impressive thing Ted showed that year was patience and discipline in the batter's box. In 565 trips to the plate, he struck out just 64 times. In 1939, he was facing major league pitchers for the first time. He had never seen them throw before. They were the best pitchers in the world. If he could handle them as a rookie, what would he be able to do after gaining some experience?

Many slick-hitting rookies have faded toward the end of their seasons. In most cases, major league pitchers are able to find a weakness in a rookie's swing. But Ted was never intimidated by pitchers. Whenever he fell behind in the count, he focused even more. He could usually stop himself from swinging at a bad pitch. He was able to foul the tough ones off or put them into play. If a pitcher made the mistake of leaving a ball out over the plate, it would usually end up in the right field seats. Ted was almost always able to protect the strike zone.

Ted impressed a lot of people that first season. Red Sox owner Tom Yawkey was no exception. He was so enthusiastic about Ted that he restructured Fenway Park to complement his swing. Yawkey arranged to have the right field fence moved in twenty feet. Now Ted didn't have to hit the ball perfectly to knock it out of Fenway. With the fence just 380 feet away, Ted could get under one and still hit it out. With the new dimensions, a ball that wouldn't make it to the warning track with Fenway's 1939 dimensions would sail over the fence with room to spare.

# 1940

The year 1940 was a bit tougher for Ted. Early in the season, the Red Sox jumped out to a 17-6 record and led the New York Yankees by two games. But it was short-lived glory. By July, the Sox had fallen apart. By the end of the summer, their pennant hopes were pretty much over. The Sox finished with an 82-72 record, tied for fourth with the Chicago White Sox, eight games out of first place.

As a left-handed hitter, Williams took advantage of the fact that he was always one step closer to first base than a right-hander.

The shallower fences in right field seemed to work against Ted. He hit just 23 home runs that year, one of the lowest home run totals in his career. Ted was able to raise his batting average in his second year to hit .344, a fine percentage for a second-year player. He drove in 113 runs and struck out just 54 times in 561 trips to the plate.

His performance on the field had been good but not spectacular. Red Sox fans were expecting Ted to rule the world that year. The pressure might have been too great. He may have been trying too hard to hit home runs.

## Ted's Reputation

Ted's off-the-field problems were bigger than his on-the-field problems in 1940. Boston sportswriters cemented Ted's reputation that year. From then on, the baseball world would perceive him as an ill-tempered, angry man.

The biggest Ted Williams news story was when Ted asked Coach Cronin for a day off. The request came at the end of a horrible July, when the Red Sox couldn't even buy a win. Ted told

Cronin he needed a day to rest his sore back. Around the same time, Boston slugger Jimmie Foxx asked Cronin for a day off because his four-year-old son was having his tonsils removed.

Cronin was fed up with his team's lack of commitment. He hinted to a Boston sports-writer that he would have the team doctor check on Ted's back before giving him time off.

Cronin would never have done this to Foxx, who was an established veteran. Ted, at only twenty-one years old, was still a kid in the eyes of the older Cronin.

Cronin didn't think it was a big deal. Foxx would be out of the lineup, so he would really need Ted.

When the doctor went to check him, Ted became livid.

Ted screamed and flailed his arms when reporters asked him about the injury. He blamed everyone around him as being part of a conspiracy to ruin him. He blamed his team-mates, his coaches, and the people of Boston. He blamed the city of Boston itself—its streets, its trees, and the cold climate.

*The Globe*'s headline for the story on Ted's outburst read "Ted Williams is a grown man with the mind of a juvenile."

The *New York Post* published a story by writer Jack Miley that said, "If his noodle swells another inch, Master Ted Williams won't be able to get his hat on with a shoehorn."

# Batting .406

**B**aseball is a game of numbers. So much depends on statistics. It is impossible to talk about baseball without talking about statistics. Statistics are the numbers used to determine a player's greatness and worthiness for earning a place in the Major League Baseball Hall of Fame in Cooperstown, New York. As an example, the number 500 is a huge Hall of Fame indicator. Any player who hits 500 home runs over his career is almost guaranteed entry into the Hall of Fame.

Another important number is .300. Players strive to hit .300. It's pretty much accepted that good hitters will be able to manage at least three hits for every ten chances they have at the plate. So if a player hits .300 over the course of a season, it is generally said that he had a good year.

In the Baseball Hall of Fame in Cooperstown, New York, Joe DiMaggio's plaque wears a wreath of flowers to mourn his passing in March of 1999. Although he acknowledged that he himself was the better hitter, Williams considered DiMaggio the best all-around player who ever lived.

To hit .400 is nearly impossible. But in 1941, Ted hit .406! More than sixty major league seasons have come and gone, yet no other ballplayer has reached the .400 mark since 1941.

Other hitting milestones have fallen over the years, but Ted's still stand.

Roger Maris broke Babe Ruth's single-season home run record in 1961 by hitting 61 home runs, breaking the Babe's previous record of 60. People said that his record would never be broken. But Mark McGwire shattered the record in 1998 when he hit a whopping 70 home runs. McGwire's record was topped just three years later, in 2001, when Barry Bonds smashed a Herculean 73 long balls.

As people learn more and more about strength training, players are getting stronger and stronger. Team fitness trainers know how to structure workouts to increase a hitter's power. If this trend continues, it might be realistic to predict that a player will hit 100 home runs in a single season sometime soon.

But it seems unlikely that a player will hit .400 ever again. It requires an incredible amount of talent and a lion's share of luck. Great hitters in their best seasons rarely come close to .400. George Brett hit .390 for the Kansas City Royals in 1980. Tony Gwynn hit .394 for the San Diego Padres in 1994. Larry Walker hit .379 for the Colorado Rockies in 1999.

Ted was also the youngest player to ever hit .400. Ted turned twenty-three in 1941. Ty

Ty Cobb, elected to the Baseball Hall of Fame in 1936, was famous for his ruthless competitive streak. Cobb hit over .400 three times in his twenty-four-season playing career, also winning twelve batting titles—the first at age twenty.

Cobb, who many people say was the best ballplayer who ever lived, was twenty-four when he hit .420 in 1911.

Ted probably wasn't thinking much about numbers at the beginning of the 1941 season. He went zero for three on May 2, and his average dropped to .308. But Ted went on a tear after that, and his average had skyrocketed to .404 by May 25. He stayed at or above the .400 mark for most of the 1941 season. His average dipped into the .390s in mid-July, but he fought back and had his average up to .39955 on the last day of the season.

The Red Sox were scheduled to play a doubleheader in Philadelphia against the Athletics. If Ted sat out, his average would have been rounded up to .400. Ted had the batting title wrapped up. The second-place hitter, Cecil Travis of the Washington Senators, was hitting .359 and having the best year of his career. Even so, he had no chance of catching Williams.

Instead of sitting the bench and entering the history books with his incredible .400 average, Ted wanted to push it up a few points.

It was a gamble. Because his average was already so high, he would need a nearly perfect game to raise it. If he went one for three, two for six, or even three for eight over the two games, his average would fall beneath .400.

Before the game, Athletics coach Al Simmons came into the Boston dugout. Simmons had hit .380 twice in his career. He had always believed Ted was too picky at the plate. Simmons thought Ted could have been more productive if

Ted Williams stares down a Yankee pitcher in 1941, the year he batted .406. Always bitter rivals with the Yankees, the Red Sox have been unable to claim a World Series title since 1918.

he swung the bat more. He said to Ted, "How much you wanna bet you don't hit .400?"

Simmons was trying to rattle him. He was trying to make him nervous. But it was a strategy that never seemed to work on Ted. He always played better when the odds were against him, when people doubted him.

So Ted took his chances and went six for eight in the doubleheader. He hit a home run and raised his average to .406.

# Second Fiddle

Baseball writers weren't impressed. They gave the Most Valuable Player Award to Joe DiMaggio of the New York Yankees. DiMaggio had hit .357 that year and had set his own major league record—a fifty-six-game hitting streak. DiMaggio's record still stands. There have been just two serious attempts at breaking DiMaggio's hitting streak record. In 1978, Pete Rose hit safely in forty-four consecutive games for the Cincinnati Reds. Paul Molitor hit in thirty-nine consecutive games for the Milwaukee Brewers in 1987.

Ted's .406 average didn't break any records, but it put him at number nineteen on the all-time single-season batting average list.

Unfortunately for Ted, opinions about a player's personality sway sportswriters when they vote for the MVP. DiMaggio was thought of as a friendly person and a hero. Two hit songs have been written about DiMaggio. He married Marilyn Monroe, Hollywood's most glamorous actress in the 1950s. Ted was thought of as a cold, callous, bitter man.

Ted Williams smiles with the much-beloved Joe DiMaggio at Fenway Park, right before the first game of the 1950 season.

In general, people liked DiMaggio and disliked Ted Williams. While Ted was a better hitter, DiMaggio was regarded by many as the better player. The numbers don't lie: Ted hit .344 with 521 home runs and 1,839 runs batted in over 19 seasons. DiMaggio hit .325 with 361 home runs and 1,537 RBIs in 15 seasons. But because of public opinion, DiMaggio won the MVP Award three times, and Ted won it only twice.

In 1942, Ted won the American League Triple Crown Award. He led the American League in the three most important offensive categories: batting average, home runs, and RBIs. Even though Ted hit .356 with 36 home runs and 137 RBIs, Ted finished second to Joe Gordon, who hit .322 with just 18 home runs for the Yankees that year. Numbers show that Ted had played a better year, but was being snubbed by the media.

## World War II

The infamous sneak attack on Pearl Harbor and the United States's official entrance into World War II overshadowed Ted's unbelievable 1941 baseball season. More than 3,400 people died on December 7, 1941, when Japan attacked the Pearl Harbor Naval Station in Hawaii, drawing the United States into the worldwide conflict.

Ted, like most ballplayers, knew he would be drafted into the U.S. military while he played the 1942 season. In January 1942, Ted received a notice from the U.S. military announcing that he could be drafted at any time. The only question was when.

With a solemn face, Williams enlists in the navy to fight the Axis forces on May 22, 1942. He was later assigned to the marines. Although he flew many missions in the Korean War, Williams would not see any combat during World War II.

It was a strange time for baseball as fans tried to cling to the sport as a way to divert their attention from the horror and tragedy of the world. As it came to light that Hitler was bent on destroying all of Europe's Jewish population, people questioned the importance of baseball. How could grown men play a game when they were needed in the war effort?

Ted fought with the idea. He had his draft status reclassified so there would be less likelihood of him being drafted. Ted was the sole supporter of his mother, May. He could not support her if he went to fight in the war. The Boston press tore into him, accusing him of being unpatriotic.

Ted enlisted in the armed forces in May 1942. He signed up for the U.S. Navy's aviation program, but was assigned to the marines. He took flight-training classes while slugging his way to the 1942 Triple Crown Award.

Ted was called into service in November. When he underwent his physical, military doctors discovered that he had 20/10 vision. This meant he could see at twenty feet away

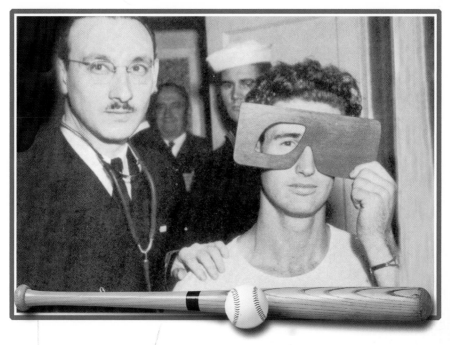

During Ted Williams's military physical in 1942, doctors discovered that he had extraordinary 20/10 vision. This may have helped him set many student records during his pilot training for flight maneuvers, reflexes, and visual reaction time, among others.

what someone with regular 20/20 vision could only see at ten feet away.

Ted was actually upset about this. People often said that hitting the ball came easy for him because he had superhuman eyesight. Ted imagined that his ability to see the ball came from hard work and practice. But his eyesight was, in fact, extraordinary.

In his 1969 autobiography, *My Turn at Bat*, Ted said, "They used to write a lot of bull

Williams wears his navy cadet's uniform while his fiancée, Doris Soule, smiles at him in this July 14, 1943, photo. Their ill-fated marriage ended twelve years later.

about my eyesight. Sure, I think I had good eyesight, maybe exceptional eyesight, but not superhuman eyesight."

Ted's extraordinary eyesight was a blessing over the next few years. It helped him through naval flight school. Ted went on to basic flight training at Bunker Hill Naval Air Station in Kokomo, Indiana. From there he moved on to Pensacola, Florida, for advanced flight training. He became a flight instructor in Pensacola and learned to fly the SNJ, a combat fighter with a top speed of 205 miles per hour.

Ted earned the rank of second lieutenant in 1944. He married Doris Soule of Princeton, Minnesota, that year. Ted and Doris had a baby girl, Bobby Jo, in 1948. They were divorced in 1955. In all, Williams would marry three times and have three children.

Ted set a student gunnery record in Jacksonville, Florida. He learned to fly the F4U Corsair, a fighter with a top speed of 445 miles per hour. On August 15, 1945, Ted was sent by the marines to Hawaii. But he received his orders to return home shortly after he arrived there.

Ted gave three years in the prime of his career to the U.S. military, but never saw combat.

## Back to Baseball

When Ted returned to the baseball field after the war, he picked up right where he had left off. Ted led the league in several offensive categories, won his first MVP Award, and led the Red Sox to the 1946 World Series.

The Red Sox had their last great season in 1946. They dominated the American League that year. They won 104 games and lost just 50. They finished twelve games ahead of second-place Detroit and seventeen games ahead of their arch rival, the New York Yankees. The Sox have not had a 100-win season since.

The Red Sox squared off against the St. Louis Cardinals in the 1946 World Series. The first two games of the series were played at Sportsman's Park in St. Louis. The Sox won the first game 3–2 and got shut out 3–0 in Game 2. The Sox had managed just four hits in Game 2.

The Sox won Game 3 and lost Game 4, tying the series at two games apiece. A three-run

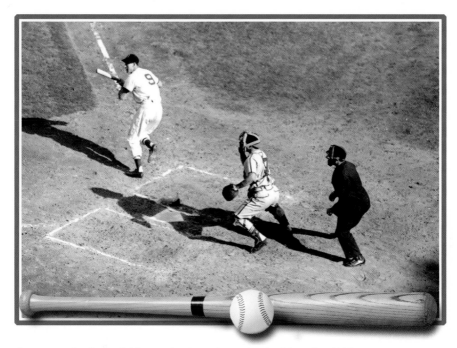

Surprising Cardinal infielders with a bunt down the third base line, Williams runs to first while catcher Joe Garagiola scrambles for the ball during Game 3 of the 1946 World Series.

seventh inning homer helped the Sox to a victory in Game 5, putting the World Series in their favor three games to two. Ted managed a single and his only run batted in of the series in Game 5.

If you know baseball, you know how this ends. The Sox lost Game 6 by a 4–1 score. They rallied with 2 runs in the top of the eighth inning of Game 7, but St. Louis came back with a run in the bottom of the eighth and won it 4–3. The Sox had lost the World Series.

Because of his tendency to pull the ball to the right, the Cardinals infield shifts as Williams steps up to the plate during Game 2 of the 1946 World Series. Ty Cobb often remarked that Williams would have had an even higher batting average if he had been able to hit consistently to left field.

Ted had flopped. It may have been the cold climate that held him down, because the pressure to win had always made Ted stronger. Ted hit just .200 in the 1946 World Series. He had no home runs, doubles, or triples, and just one run batted in. He walked five times and struck out five times. He had always struggled in chilly weather. October nights in Boston and St. Louis can get pretty nippy. It was a letdown, because the Red Sox really needed his bat.

The 1946 playoff was one of the last shots the Red Sox would have to win the World Series for thirty years. They had a great team again in 1986, but they ended up losing both World Series in seven games. The Red Sox have not won a World Series since 1918.

# Korea,
# Coaching, and
# the Hall of Fame

T ed overpowered American League pitchers between 1947 and 1951. Over those five seasons, he averaged .338, with 32 home runs and 124 runs batted in. But 1951 was the last time he would score or drive in 100 runs.

## The Korean War

Ted's attention in 1952 was focused on serving his country. He missed 150 games between 1952 and 1953 to serve as an F-9 fighter jet pilot in the Korean War.

Ted returned to active duty and reported to Cherry Point, North Carolina. In May 1952, the SNV he had flown during World War II was pretty much outdated. He took a refresher course on the basics of flying and learned how to fly an F-9.

Already a veteran of World War II, Williams gives the thumbs-up to his mechanic while training to fly a Corsair fighter plane on September 4, 1952.

In *Ted Williams: A Baseball Life*, Williams is quoted as saying that F-9s were easy to fly. They were much more advanced than the prop-based fighter planes he had flown during World War II.

Unlike the time he spent in WWII, his time served during the Korean War was spent attacking the enemy. Ted had never made it into combat during WWII; the war was nearly over by the time he finished basic training. Korea was different. U.S. draft policy prohibited the military from selecting college students. Men who had served in WWII were called on to fight again.

Ted went from Cherry Point to operational training at Roosevelt Roads in the Sierra Nevada mountains. Training was tough. Ted and his outfit lived off of canned food rations. They slept outdoors and used their parachutes as tents.

He arrived in Korea as a member of the Third Marines Air Wing, 223rd Squadron. After a few practice runs, he entered into combat.

There were some very close calls.

On February 17, 1953, Ted lost sight of the plane in front of him. He was flying over his target during an air mission against Kyomipo, North Korea.

He brought his plane too low and got hit by North Korean soldiers who fired at him from the ground. His plane caught fire, and he lost his landing gear and his communications. Ted was somehow able to land the plane safely. He was sent on another mission the very next day.

Ted's plane was hit again in April. The marines were engaged in an air raid on the western coast of Korea. Ted was again flying low to the ground. His plane was hit by Korean fire. He was lucky to make it back safely to his base.

Ted flew thirty-nine missions in Korea. "I was no hero," Ted is quoted on the official Ted Williams Web site (http://www.tedwilliams.com). "There were maybe seventy-five pilots in our two squadrons and 99 percent of them did a better job than I did."

Because cold weather always got the best of him, Ted ended up spending more time in the infirmary than in his jet. He came down with pneumonia and spent several weeks on a hospital ship. Doctors discovered an ear problem, and Ted was no longer able to fly. Ted was honorably discharged in July 1953.

## Baseball Re-revisited

After Korea, Ted returned to the Red Sox. He had given up nearly two more years to serve his country.

Ted hit well above .300 every year between 1954 and 1960, when he retired. His most impressive years were 1957 and 1958. Ted led the American League with a .388 average in 1957, ahead of second-place Mickey Mantle, whose average was .328 that year. Ted was forty years old when he took the 1958 batting title. While few pro athletes play sports into their forties, Ted was still the best hitter in the league.

Not wanting to be forgotten, Ted crushed a home run in his very last major league at bat. The ball flew over the right field fence in Boston and landed in the Red Sox bullpen. He helped the Sox win the game, 5–4.

## Coach Williams

After playing his last game in 1960, Ted left baseball for nine years. He returned in 1969 when Bob Short, owner of the Washington Senators, asked Ted to manage his ballclub.

Ted accepted the offer.

In his first year as Senators manager, Ted led the team to an 86-76 record. Annual attendance at home games increased by 400,000.

The Senators were always thought of as a second-rate expansion ballclub. In 1969 they

Although the Washington Senators did not last long as a baseball team, Williams won the American League Manager of the Year Award in 1969 for his work with the team.

had their only winning season. In ten years, the team compiled a 740-1032 record.

The team had finished at 65-96, thirty-two games under .500 the year before Ted took control. They had hit just .224 as a team and scored just 524 runs.

In 1969, with Ted as their coach, they hit .254 and scored 694 runs. Ted earned American League Manager of the Year honors for turning the team around. Under Ted's leadership, Washington slugger Frank Howard reached his career high in batting (.296) and home runs (48). Howard finished fourth in MVP voting that year.

The Senators struggled in Washington, and owner Bob Short sold several of his best players before the 1970 season began. The team hit just .217 in 1971. Short moved the team to Texas and renamed them the Texas Rangers. Ted retired from the Rangers after the 1972 season, finishing his managerial career with a 273-364 record.

# The Hall of Fame

In 1966, Ted Williams was voted into the Baseball Hall of Fame. Ninety-three percent of those

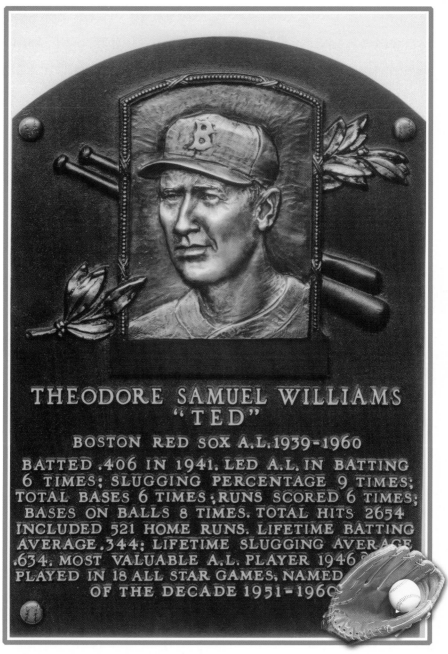

THEODORE SAMUEL WILLIAMS
"TED"

BOSTON RED SOX A.L. 1939-1960

BATTED .406 IN 1941. LED A.L. IN BATTING
6 TIMES; SLUGGING PERCENTAGE 9 TIMES;
TOTAL BASES 6 TIMES; RUNS SCORED 6 TIMES;
BASES ON BALLS 8 TIMES. TOTAL HITS 2654
INCLUDED 521 HOME RUNS. LIFETIME BATTING
AVERAGE .344; LIFETIME SLUGGING AVERAGE
.634. MOST VALUABLE A.L. PLAYER 1946
PLAYED IN 18 ALL STAR GAMES. NAMED
OF THE DECADE 1951-1960

On July 25, 1966, after many years of excellence in the major leagues, Ted Williams was immortalized in the Baseball Hall of Fame.

voting gave him the thumbs-up. Ted had hit some of the most majestic home runs ever seen. He had earned two Triple Crown Awards, two MVP Awards, six American League batting championships, eighteen selections to the American League All Star team, and a lifetime batting average of .344. He had hit 521 home runs.

Ted's career spanned twenty-one years. His 1941 season earned him a reputation as one of the best hitters ever to play the game. He hit .406 that season. No one has hit for a better average in the sixty-plus years that have come and gone since then.

He could have put up even more impressive numbers if two wars hadn't forced him to spend five years in the U.S. military.

In retirement, Ted became an excellent fly-fisherman. Ted opened the Hitters Hall of Fame in Hernando, Florida, where he lived.

After being in ill health, Ted Williams died of a heart attack in 2002. Thousands of fans gathered at Fenway Park to say goodbye to the greatest hitter who ever lived.

# Ted Williams's Statistics

| Year | G | AB | H | HR | R | RBI | BB | SO | Avg | Slg |
|------|-----|------|------|-----|------|------|------|-----|------|------|
| 1939 | 149 | 565 | 185 | 31 | 131 | *145* | 107 | 64 | .327 | .609 |
| 1940 | 144 | 561 | 193 | 23 | 134 | 113 | 96 | 54 | .344 | .594 |
| 1941 | 143 | 456 | 185 | *37* | *135* | 120 | *145* | 27 | *.406* | *.735* |
| 1942 | 150 | 522 | 186 | *36* | *141* | 137 | *145* | 51 | *.356* | *.648* |
| 1946 | 150 | 514 | 176 | 38 | *142* | 123 | *156* | 44 | .342 | *.667* |
| 1947 | 156 | 528 | 181 | *32* | *125* | *114* | *162* | 47 | *.343* | *.634* |
| 1948 | 137 | 509 | 188 | 25 | 124 | 127 | *126* | 41 | .369 | *.615* |
| 1949 | *155* | 566 | 194 | *43* | *150* | *159* | *162* | 48 | .343 | *.650* |
| 1950 | 89 | 334 | 106 | 28 | 82 | 97 | 82 | 21 | .317 | .647 |
| 1951 | 148 | 531 | 169 | 30 | 109 | 126 | 144 | 45 | .318 | .556 |
| 1952 | 6 | 10 | 4 | 1 | 2 | 3 | 2 | 2 | .400 | .90 |
| 1953 | 37 | 91 | 37 | 13 | 17 | 34 | 19 | 10 | .407 | .90 |
| 1954 | 117 | 386 | 133 | 29 | 93 | 89 | *136* | 32 | .345 | *.635* |
| 1955 | 98 | 320 | 114 | 28 | 77 | 83 | 91 | 24 | .356 | .703 |
| 1956 | 136 | 400 | 138 | 24 | 71 | 82 | 102 | 39 | .345 | .605 |
| 1957 | 132 | 420 | 163 | 38 | 96 | 87 | 119 | 43 | .388 | .731 |
| 1958 | 129 | 411 | 135 | 26 | 81 | 85 | 98 | 49 | *.328* | .584 |
| 1959 | 103 | 272 | 69 | 10 | 32 | 43 | 52 | 27 | .254 | .419 |
| 1960 | 113 | 310 | 98 | 29 | 56 | 72 | 75 | 41 | .316 | .645 |
| **Total** | **2292** | **7706** | **2654** | **521** | **1798** | **1839** | **2019** | **709** | **.344** | **.634** |

*Bold italic indicates a statistic in which Ted led the American League for that year.

97

# TED WILLIAMS *TIMELINE*

| | | |
|---|---|---|
| ⚾ | **Aug. 30 1918** | Theodore Samuel Williams is born in San Diego, California. |
| ⚾ | **June 26 1936** | Ted signs his first professional baseball contract with the San Diego Padres. |
| ⚾ | **1937** | Ted hits 23 home runs in his first full professional season and signs a minor league contract with the Boston Red Sox after the season is over. |
| ⚾ | **1938** | Ted plays his first game with the Minneapolis Millers. |
| ⚾ | **1939** | Ted makes his major league debut with the Boston Red Sox. |
| ⚾ | **1940** | The right field fence at Fenway Park in Boston is shortened to 380 feet to complement Ted's swing. Ted plays in his first Major League All Star Game. |
| ⚾ | **1941** | Ted hits .406 for the season. No player in baseball has hit over .400 since since 1941. |
| ⚾ | **Dec. 7 1941** | Japan launches a sneak attack on Pearl Harbor. The attack draws the U.S. into World War II. |
| ⚾ | **1942** | Ted wins the Triple Crown Award by leading the American League in batting home runs and RBIs. |
| ⚾ | **Nov. 1942** | Ted is called into active service with the U.S. military. |
| ⚾ | **1944** | Ted earns the rank of second lieutenant with the U.S. Marines. He marries Doris Soule. They divorce in 1955. |

| | | |
|---|---|---|
| ⚾ | **August 1945** | Atomic bombs are dropped on Hiroshima and Nagasaki, Japan. |
| ⚾ | **1946** | Ted wins the American League Most Valuable Player Award and leads the Red Sox to the 1946 World Series. The Sox lose the series three games to four. |
| ⚾ | **1947** | Ted wins his second American League Triple Crown Award. He bats .343 with 32 home runs and 114 RBIs. |
| ⚾ | **1948** | Ted leads the American League with a .369 batting average. His daughter, Bobby Jo, is born. |
| ⚾ | **1951** | Ted plays in his ninth All Star Game. He leads the American League with 295 total bases, 144 walks, and a .556 slugging percentage. |
| ⚾ | **1952** | Ted returns to active duty with the U.S. Marines and learns to pilot the F-9 fighter jet. |
| ⚾ | **Feb. 17 1954** | Ted is nearly killed in combat when his plane is hit by enemy fire, but he lands safely. |
| ⚾ | **1954** | Ted returns to major league baseball, batting .345 with 29 home runs and 89 RBIs in just 113 games. |
| ⚾ | **1966** | Ted is elected into the Major League Baseball Hall of Fame. |
| ⚾ | **1969** | Ted writes *My Turn At Bat*. He begins coaching the Washington Senators baseball club. |
| ⚾ | **1972** | Ted retires from coaching the Senators and immerses himself in fly-fishing. |
| ⚾ | **2002** | Ted Williams dies. |

# Glossary

**at bat** One chance at the plate.

**Baseball Hall of Fame** A complex in Cooperstown, New York, where baseball's finest players are honored.

**benched** To be taken out of the starting lineup and seated on the bench in the dugout.

**breaking ball** A curveball or slider. These pitches break downward as they approach the plate.

**cavalry** Military troops trained to fight on horseback.

**concentration camps** Camps where prisoners are jailed, tortured, or executed.

**double** A hit that enables a batter to run safely to second base.

**doubleheader**   Two games played by the same two teams in the same day.

**double play**   A play that allows the defense to record two outs off of a single batted ball. Most double plays result when the batter hits a ground ball to shortstop or second base when there is a runner on first. The defense will usually throw the ball to second to force out the runner coming in from first base, then throw out the batter heading to first base to complete the double play.

**exploits**   Acts and deeds, sometimes outrageous.

**genocide**   The systematic, premeditated extermination of an entire racial, political, national, ethnic, or religious group.

**Great Depression**   A period following the stock market crash of 1929. Many Americans lost everything they owned and had a very hard time earning money to buy food or pay rent.

**grounder**   A hit baseball that travels low to the ground.

**home run**   A ball hit over the fence. The

batter and all runners on base touch home plate and score.

**long ball**   Slang for home run.

**MVP**   Most Valuable Player.

**pennant**   A small tapering flag. The pennant represents the baseball championship. The winners of the American League pennant and National League pennant meet in the World Series.

**pinch hitter**   A hitter brought in to replace someone in the starting lineup. Pinch hitters are usually called upon late in games in order to get better matchups against the opposition.

**press**   Newspaper writers and editors.

**punched out**   A term for the action made by the home plate umpire when he calls a batter out on strikes. Many umpires pump their fists in the air.

**RBI**   A run batted in.

**Salvation Army**   A not-for-profit religious organization that offers shelter for the homeless, food for the hungry, alcohol and drug counseling, plus other community services.

**shagging**   Catching fly balls during practice.

**single**   A hit in which the batter safely reaches first base.

**strike out**   An at bat where a batter either swings and misses at a third strike or is called out on a third strike crossing over the plate.

**to fan**   To strike out.

**triple**   A hit in which the batter runs safely to third base.

**veteran**   A player who has had several years of major league experience; also a person who has served in the military.

**walk**   When a pitcher delivers four balls out of the strike zone that the batter lets go by, the batter is awarded a walk to first base.

**warning track**   A dirt path that lies between the edge of the outfield grass and the outfield fence.

# For More Information

The Jimmy Fund
  10 Brookline Place West
  5th Floor
  Brookline, MA 02445-7295
  (800) 52-JIMMY (525-4669)
  Web site:http://www.jimmyfund.org/
     contactus.asp

  National Baseball Hall of Fame
  and Museum
  25 Main Street
  P.O. Box 590
  Cooperstown, NY 13326
  (888) HALL-OF-FAME (425-5633)
Web site: http://www.baseballhalloffame.org

Save Fenway, Inc.

P.O. Box 873

Boston, MA 02103

(617) 367-3771

Web site: http://www.savefenwaypark.com/
    contact.cfm

The Society for American Baseball
    Research (SABR)

812 Huron Road

Suite 719

Cleveland, OH 44115

(216) 575-0500

Web site: http://www.sabr.org

Ted Williams League Headquarters

P.O. Box 1127

Pembroke, MA 02359

(800) 895-8925

Web site: http://www.twmuseum.com/aboutus/
    ted_williams_league.html

**Ted Williams Retrospective Museum &**
        **Library, Inc.**
2455 North Citrus Hills Boulevard
Hernando, FL 34442
(352) 527-6566
Web site: http://www.twmuseum.com

## Web Sites

Due to the changing nature of Internet links, the Rosen Publishing Group, Inc., has developed an online list of Web sites related to the subject of this book. This site is updated regularly. Please use this link to access the list:

http://www.rosenlinks.com/bhf/twim/

# For Further Reading

Cataneo, David. *I Remember Ted Williams: Anecdotes and Memories of Baseball's Splendid Splinter by the Players and People Who Knew Him*. Nashville, TN: Cumberland House, 2002.

Rainbolt, Richard. *Baseball's Home-Run Hitters*. Minneapolis, MN: Lerner Publications Co., 1975.

Sampson, Arthur. *Ted Williams: A Biography of The Kid*. New York: Barnes, 1959.

Schoor, Gene, and Henry Gifford. *The Ted Williams Story*. New York: J. Messner, 1954.

Williams, Ted, and David Pietrusza. *Ted Williams: My Life in Pictures*. Kingston, NY: Total/Sports Illustrated, 2001.

# Bibliography

Baldassaro, Lawrence, ed. *The Ted Williams Reader*. New York: Fireside, 1991.

BaseballReference.com. "Ted Williams" and "Boston Red Sox." Retrieved March 24, 2002 (http://www. baseballreference.com).

Blood, Ted. *The Splendid Splinter: The Story of How the Sportswriters Tried to Chop Up the Splinter for Firewood*. New York: Exposition Press, 1960.

Linn, Ed. *Hitter: The Life and Turmoils of Ted Williams*. New York: Harcourt Brace Jovanovich & Co., 1993.

The Official Ted Williams Website. "World War II" and "Korean War." Retrieved May 11, 2002 (http://www.tedwilliams.com).

Pope, Edwin. *Ted Williams: The Golden Year 1957*. Englewood Cliffs, NJ: Prentice-Hall, Inc., 1970.

Seidel, Michael. *Ted Williams: A Baseball Life*. Chicago, IL: Contemporary Books, Inc., 1991.

Williams, Ted, and John Underwood. *My Turn At Bat: The Story of My Life*. Rev. ed. New York: Simon & Schuster, 1988.

Williams, Ted, and John Underwood. *The Science of Hitting*. New York: Simon and Schuster, 1971.

# Index

## About the Author

Shaun McCormack, a graduate of Montclair State University, is a writer living in New Jersey. A baseball lover since age five, when his grandfather took him to see a game for the first time, Shaun has also written *Cool Papa Bell* and *Willie Mays* for the Rosen Publishing Group, Inc.

## Photo Credits

Cover © Hulton Archive/Getty Images; pp. 4, 16, 20, 30, 43, 46, 59, 95 © Bettmann/Corbis; p. 7 © Michael Maslan Historic Photographs/ Corbis; p. 9 © Underwood & Underwood/ Corbis; p. 13 © San Diego Hall of Champions; pp. 22, 26, 36, 39, 50, 53, 60, 65, 70, 72, 74, 76, 78–79, 82, 85, 86, 89, 93 © AP/Wide World Photos; p. 55 © Leonard McCombe/Timepix; p. 81 courtesy of Ted Williams Family Enterprises, LTD.

## Editor

Jill Jarnow

## Series Design and Layout

Geri Giordano